WATCH THEM
GROW

Written by Linda Martin

DORLING KINDERSLEY
LONDON • NEW YORK • STUTTGART

A DORLING KINDERSLEY BOOK

Written and edited by Linda Martin
Designer Ingrid Mason,
Editorial Consultant Theresa Greenaway
Illustrators Sandra Pond, Will Giles
Production Catherine Semark
US Assistant Editor Camela Decaire

First American Edition, 1994
2 4 6 8 10 9 7 5 3 1

Published in the United States by
Dorling Kindersley, Inc., 232 Madison Avenue
New York, New York 10016

ISBN 1-56458-458-5

Library of Congress Cataloging-in-Publication Data is available for this title.

Color reproduction by Colourscan, Singapore

Printed and bound in Italy by L.E.G.O.

Contents

All sorts of babies

Many baby animals and plants change as they grow. What do you think these babies will look like when they grow up?

1

2

3

(Answers on page 45)

5

4

6

7

8

9

10

9

Being born

Can you guess what these baby animals will grow into? See if you can match them up with their mothers on the next page.

1

2

3

4

Each one of these baby animals feeds on its mother's milk. They are all mammals.

5

6

Sheep

Dog

Tiger

Wolf

All these grown-up animals are furry.

Kangaroo

Rabbit

(Answers on page 45)

Cat

A baby cat is called a kitten. A kitten looks sort of scruffy when it is born. But watch this one grow into a sleek, silky cat like its mother.

1 Just born

A newborn kitten is very sleepy.

A newborn kitten is covered with fur. It cannot see or hear.

2 Eyes open

Two weeks later, a kitten can see and hear. It also starts to explore.

3 Full of fun

Kittens become more and more energetic as they grow stronger. They spend a lot of time playing.

A ball of yarn is one of a kitten's favorite toys.

4 All grown up

This kitten eats the same food as its parents now.

At ten weeks old, a kitten is a young cat. It has grown a lot, hasn't it? But it needs to grow even more before it can have kittens of its own.

 # Rabbit

A baby rabbit is very strange-looking!
It is bald and wrinkly – not a bit like a cuddly grown-up rabbit.

1 Just born

A newborn rabbit does not have any fur. Its eyes are shut and it cannot hear. It is very sleepy.

2 Soft fur

Soft fur has started to grow. But a rabbit's eyes are still shut and it cannot hear yet.

3 Looking for adventure

Now that this rabbit can see and hear, it starts to explore. It doesn't wander too far away though.

This grass looks good enough to eat!

Eating lots of lettuce will help it grow big and strong.

4 Long ears

This young rabbit is six weeks old and is much bigger. Look how its ears have grown! It is very cuddly now, isn't it?

15

Dog

A baby dog is called a puppy. A puppy grows quite slowly. It takes more than a year for a puppy to grow as big as its mother.

1 Just born

A newborn puppy cannot see or hear.

A puppy is born with lots of fur. It only wakes up when it is hungry!

2 Eyes open

A puppy's nose is very short.

A puppy walks around as soon as it can see where it is going!

3 Playful pup

As a puppy grows, it spends more and more time playing. Its fur is thick and fluffy now.

4 A young dog

This puppy is eight weeks old and looks much more like a grown-up dog. Its tail and ears have grown longer.

This puppy's face has grown longer, too.

Horse

A baby horse is called a foal. Apart from being much smaller, a foal looks a lot like its mother when it is born.

1 Long legs

A foal runs about on its long legs soon after being born.

A foal can see and hear when it is born.

2 Growing up

A foal grows bigger and stronger every day.

3 Munching apples

A growing foal gallops around the fields to stretch its legs. This makes it very hungry. It eats apples as well as grass now.

4 Filling out

The foal's body and legs are fatter, too.

This foal is five months old. Its coat is shiny brown and its tail and mane have grown much longer. It will be at least another year before it is as big as its mother though.

Eggs

Some baby animals hatch from eggs. Do you think you can guess what will hatch from these eggs? Look for their mothers on the next page.

1

2

3

4

5

6

Spider

Duck

Owl

Dogfish

Snake

Lizard

(Answers on page 45)

Chicken

Watch this fluffy chick grow up to look like its father. It will look quite different from its mother.

1 Hatching

A chick hatches from an egg laid by its mother. It is very wet, isn't it?

2 Soft and fluffy

A chick's feathers are soft and fluffy. It loves to eat seeds.

3 Changing color

This chick is growing bigger. Its fluffy yellow feathers have fallen out and new gray ones have grown instead.

This chick still does not look like its father, does it?

4 Redhead

Now this chick is eight weeks old. Most of its adult feathers have grown and it has a red "comb" on its head, just like its father.

The chick's long black tail feathers have not grown yet.

 # Duck

Ducklings grow very quickly. It takes only a few weeks for this duckling to grow into a fine white duck like its mother.

1 Hatching

A duckling pushes its way out of an egg laid by its mother.

2 Splash!

After only two days, a duckling goes for its first swim. It loves it!

3 New feathers

This duckling is changing shape. It is not as round as it was before. Its baby feathers are falling out. New white feathers are growing in their place.

4 Fine wings

This duckling's short yellow beak has grown into a long orange one.

This duckling is six weeks old. All its feathers are white and its wings are big and strong. Soon it will fly for the first time.

Parrot

Look at this funny chick! Will it really grow into a green parrot like its father? Its mother is red and blue.

1 Just hatched

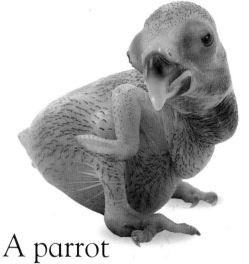

A parrot has no feathers at all when it hatches.

2 Fluffy fellow

Feathers are growing now. But they are gray!

3 Going green

This parrot chick is four weeks old. Green feathers are beginning to grow now.

The green feathers show that this chick is male.

The young parrot's long tail feathers still have to grow.

4 Almost a grown-up

This young parrot is eight weeks old. It has lost all its fluffy gray feathers. Isn't it amazing that this fine fellow could grow from that funny, bald chick?

Frog

Some creatures that hatch out of eggs look nothing like their parents! See how a tadpole grows into a frog.

1 Hatching

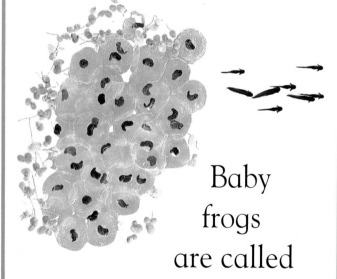

Baby frogs are called tadpoles. They hatch from eggs laid in water.

2 Eating

Tadpoles eat all the time. They grow fatter and rounder every day.

3 Growing legs

Tiny legs begin to grow. The back legs grow first, then the front legs.

4 Vanishing tail

As a tadpole's legs grow longer, its tail gets shorter and shorter.

5 Little frog

A little frog slowly grows up to look like its parents. It uses its strong back legs to jump around.

This little frog is three months old. It has lost its tail, but still has to grow a lot.

Fish

Some fish hatch from eggs. These baby fish are sticklebacks. They take two years to grow into adults like their mother and father.

1 Fish eggs

The brown mother fish lays lots of eggs in the water.

2 Tiny fish

The father fish looks after the tiny fish when they hatch.

3 Young fish

The young fish
soon grow bigger.
They eat small
shrimps, insects,
and sometimes
other fish!

4 Which color?

If this fish is female,
it will turn a dull
yellow-brown like its
mother. Which color
do you think
it will be?

This growing
fish is shiny brown. If it is male,
it will turn red, blue, and silver when
it is grown up — just like its father.

Butterfly

A fat caterpillar looks very different from its mother! Watch how this one turns into a beautiful, fluttering butterfly.

1 Hatching

A caterpillar climbs out of an egg that its mother laid.

2 Growing

A caterpillar may change color, too.

Caterpillars eat and eat!

3 Changing

A cater-pillar turns into a chrysalis.

4 A new insect

Look what is crawling out. It's a butterfly!

5 Fine wings

In a hot summer, a new butterfly is ready to lay its own eggs just eight weeks after hatching.

33

Seeds

Flowers grow from seeds. So do trees, fruits, and vegetables. Seeds are all sorts of sizes, shapes, and colors – like these. Did you know that all of these are seeds?

1

2

3

What do you think these will become? Look at the next page for clues.

4

5

6

(Answers on page 45)

Pea pod

Chestnut

Strawberry

Lemon

Dandelion

Sunflower

Bean

Do you like to eat green beans? Each bean is really a seed that could grow into a whole new bean plant. It won't grow inside your tummy though!

1 Splitting skin

The root grows down into the ground.

A seed begins to grow in the ground. First its skin splits and a tiny root appears.

2 Shooting up

A shoot appears. This grows up toward the light.

Tiny rootlets grow from the main root.

3 Leaves

A shoot continues to grow upward. After it has broken through the soil, leaves appear on the stem.

4 Flowers

A bean plant grows very fast. Small red flowers open. After the petals fall off, tiny pods form.

Young bean seeds grow inside the pods. When the pods burst, the seeds fall to the ground.

Poppy

Have you ever seen a field full of poppies? Each poppy plant grows from a tiny black seed. But where does the seed come from?

1 Poppy pods

Poppy seeds are shaken from poppy pods when the wind blows.

The seeds fall to the ground.

2 Flower buds

A leafy shoot grows from each seed. Flower buds begin to form.

3 Pretty flowers

Each bud is the beginning of a poppy flower. As a bud opens, a beautiful flower unfolds.

A poppy plant has lots of buds. But each flower only lasts for one day.

4 Falling petals

After the petals fall, seed heads, called pods, form.

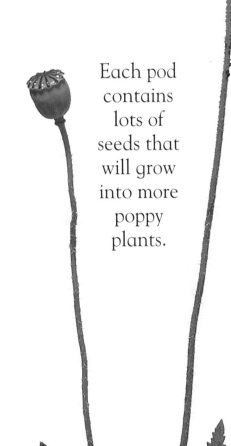

Each pod contains lots of seeds that will grow into more poppy plants.

Apple

Some very big things grow from tiny seeds. An apple tree like this takes several years to grow from a small seed.

1 Pips

The tiny pips that you see when you bite into an apple are seeds.

2 Blossoms

Pretty flowers, called blossoms, grow on apple trees.

3 Tiny apples

After a blossom falls off, tiny green apples begin to grow on the branches of the tree.

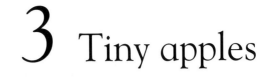

Each branch of an apple tree may be covered with growing apples.

4 Juicy fruit

Some apples turn red, some turn yellow, and others stay green.

Each little apple slowly grows into a large apple. The tasty part you eat protects the seeds inside.

Toadstool

A toadstool grows from a special kind of seed called a spore. Toadstools grow very quickly. This one grew in just one day!

1 Tiny buds

Tiny threads grow from spores underneath the ground. These threads grow into a small bud.

2 Pushing up

A bud pushes its way up out of the ground.

3 Growing up

As the stalk shoots up, the cap on top begins to open.

A toadstool cap opens out like an umbrella.

4 Fully grown

Spores are so tiny you can barely see them.

The new toadstool has flaps, called gills, underneath its cap. These gills make spores that fall to the ground.

Changes

Now you know that some babies look like their parents – apart from being smaller. Others are a different shape or color, or both!

A baby ladybug is a different color and shape.

A red pepper changes from green to red as it ripens.

A baby swan is gray, but its parents are sparkling white.

Index

Photographers: Jane Burton, Gordon Clayton, Geoff Dann, Richard Davies, Phillip Dowell, Neil Fletcher, Frank Greenaway, Dave King, Andrew McRobb, Roger Phillips, Karl Shone, Kim Taylor, Jerry Young, Barrie Watts.

Additional design assistance: Sharon Grant, Mark Haygarth, Tina Robinson

Answers from pages 8/9: 1 = Frog; 2 = Horse; 3 = Rooster; 4 = Parrot; 5 = Cuttlefish; 6 = Stickleback; 7 = Bean plant; 8 = Butterfly; 9 = Poppy plant; 10 = Cat.
Answers from pages 10/11: 1 = Tiger; 2 = Dog; 3 = Sheep; 4 = Rabbit; 5 = Wolf; 6 = Kangaroo.
Answers from pages 20/21: 1 = Spider; 2 = Duck; 3 = Dogfish; 4 = Lizard; 5 = Snake; 6 = Owl.
Answers from pages 34/35: 1 = Lemon; 2 = Pea; 3 = Sunflower; 4 = Dandelion; 5 = Strawberry; 6 = Chestnut.